## The Student's TOOLBOX

# TIPS FOR GOOD SOCIAL NETWORKING

## RUTH BENNETT

Gareth Stevens
Publishing

Please visit our website, www.garethstevens.com. For a free color catalog of all our high-quality books, call toll free 1-800-542-2595 or fax 1-877-542-2596.

Library of Congress Cataloging-in-Publication Data

Bennett, Ruth (Ruth Loetterle)
Tips for good social networking / Ruth Bennett.
    pages cm. — (The student's toolbox)
Includes index.
ISBN 978-1-4824-3296-1 (pbk.)
ISBN 978-1-4339-9958-1 (6-pack)
ISBN 978-1-4339-9957-4 (library binding)
1.  Social networks. 2.  Online social networks. 3.  Students—Social networks. 4. Students—Life skills guides.  I. Title.
HM741.B48 2014
302.3—dc23

2013028354

First Edition

Published in 2014 by
**Gareth Stevens Publishing**
111 East 14th Street, Suite 349
New York, NY 10003

© 2014 Gareth Stevens Publishing

Produced by Calcium, www.calciumcreative.co.uk
Designed by Emma Debanks and Paul Myerscough
Edited by Sarah Eason and Ronne Randall

Photo credits: Cover: Shutterstock: Ant Clausen. Inside: Dreamstime: Demonike 15, Dnf-style 16, Elenathewise 29, Michaeljung 26, Monkeybusinessimages 5, 18, 21, 22, 24, 25, Prudkov 19, Sheval 28, Stockbrokerxtra 27; Shutterstock: Blend Images 11, Sylvie Bouchard 13, Creatista 10, Andy Dean Photography 8, Hasloo Group Production Studio 7, Junial Enterprises 20, Michaeljung 23, Monkey Business Images 4, 6, 12, Sanmongkhol 1, Greg da Silva 17, Kiselev Andrey Valerevich 14, Wow 9.

Printed in the United States of America

CPSIA compliance information: Batch #CW14GS: For further information contact Gareth Stevens, New York, New York at 1-800-542-2595.

# CONTENTS

# WHAT IS SOCIAL NETWORKING?

Do you know what networking is? The fact is, you probably already network without even realizing that you're doing it! So, what is networking and why is it useful in every area of your life?

## Get Connected!

Networking is about forming connections with other people. There are plenty of ways to do this—both online and face to face. You are networking when you say hello to a neighbor on your street or when you meet someone new at a party. By connecting with people, you can learn new things, keep up to date with trends, and share your interests. Networking is a wonderful way to widen your circle of friends and find out more about the world around you. You may even find partners to work with on projects and activities you enjoy!

*Talking to your school friends is part of networking. You are networking when you share ideas and discuss the subjects you're interested in.*

## Unique Skills

Networking means that people know about you. Perhaps you are a great photographer. If the school newspaper needs some photos of an event, you would be the perfect person to take them—but first the people who run the newspaper need to know who you are! When you network, opportunities to get involved in fun and exciting projects are more likely to come your way.

**TIPS** FOR **SUCCESS**

### GETTING STARTED

To start networking, follow these simple steps:

- **Prepare:** Think about what your interests are.
- **Read:** Find places to network that match your interests. These might be online sites, community groups, or school clubs.
- **Write:** Think about how to describe yourself and your interests. You could post this description as an online profile.
- **Interact:** Go to the places you've discovered and talk to people. Find out about them and tell them about you!

# WHY NETWORK?

Why should we network? For some people, networking will just be for making new friends. Other people will want to learn more about a new hobby or make sure they find out about interesting things happening in their area.

## Take an Interest

Every person will have different networking goals. You will get the most out of your networking experience if you decide what your goals are before you start. A popular networking goal is learning from people who have more experience than you. Most people are happy to share their knowledge and will respond well if you are interested in what they do. Don't be afraid to ask people for advice!

If you're interested in finding out more about an activity, be sure to talk to the people involved.

## Get Involved

Networking is fantastic for finding activities and projects to get involved in. Be open to opportunities and you will find groups to join. If your networking goal is to put your skills to use, be sure to tell people what you have in mind. You could even think of a project that other people might want to be involved with, such as starting a band or a school recycling activity.

### TAKE NOTES

**TIPS FOR SUCCESS**

Networking involves meeting lots of different people, both online and in person. When adults network, they often categorize the information they gather to help figure out where their network might lead them. You can try this, too. Taking notes is a good way of keeping track of who is who and what they do.

7

# HOW TO NETWORK

Networking is all about exchange. Every single person in the world has unique skills and ideas. Connect with other people and share ideas with them. Tell them about you and find out about them.

## Share Your Knowledge

Meeting people is a key part of networking. Whether you are interested in photography, music, or science, finding others with the same interests is the best way to learn more and hear about opportunities. If you join a music group, for example, another member might recommend a band to you. That band might even become one of your favorites! This works both ways. There will almost certainly be a piece of music or a singer you know about that the other members don't. Why not share it with them?

There are sure to be people at school who share your interests and hobbies.

8

## Brainstorming Ideas

A great way of developing ideas is sharing them with others. Have you ever tried to figure out something on your own and gotten stuck? By sharing the problem with someone else, you are likely to find the solution. Two heads really are better than one, whether you're planning a vegetable garden or trying to identify constellations in the night sky.

### TIPS FOR SUCCESS

### LISTEN AND LEARN

Listening is an important part of networking. Think about your own ideas and what you want to say, but make sure that you listen, too. By listening, you will learn new things. Hear what other people say, and then respond. That way a conversation will develop.

# WHERE TO NETWORK

Networking can happen anywhere—at school, in the community, and online. It is always good to think about new places to network. Don't forget that every time you meet someone, you have the opportunity to network.

## Join the Club

Does your school have clubs that meet at lunchtime or after school? This is a great way to start networking. You already have something in common with others there—you all go to the same school. If the club is connected to your existing interests and hobbies, you are sure to find people who share your enthusiasm. If you are trying something new, it is an exciting beginning—who knows where it might lead?

A club or dance group is an opportunity to learn a great new skill and connect with others.

Magazines can be a good source of ideas and information when looking for groups or organizations that you could join to network.

## Eventful Meetings

You can find events in your area by looking online, checking bulletin boards, and reading your local newspaper. If you see or hear about an event that appeals to you, ask your parents if they can take you. When you are there, talk to people who are involved and find out more. It could be the beginning of a lifelong passion!

### IN THE LOOP

The Internet has made it easier than ever to access information. People often promote events on websites and social networking sites. By reading information online, you can find events that are happening in the real world.

TIPS FOR SUCCESS

# NETWORKING ONLINE

The Internet is full of opportunities for networking, and there are lots of sites especially for young people, such as YourSphere and KidzWorld. You will get the most out of networking online by using sites that are designed for kids—that way you will be connecting with other people your own age.

## All About You

Social networking is a great way to collaborate with others and share news about what you're doing. Be sure you only post things that belong to you. That means you shouldn't copy what someone else has written and pretend that it is your idea or opinion. This is called plagiarism, and it is taken very seriously—whether you're writing for fun or doing your homework.

**WARNING**

Never share personal information, such as where you live or your telephone number, online.

Post status updates to share facts and fun information with others in your social network.

Use social networking sites to keep up to date with what your friends are doing.

## So Embarrassing!

Social networking sites all have privacy settings. These are really useful as a way of controlling who can see what you post online. If your posts are visible to everyone, make sure you don't post anything that will have a negative impact on the way people see you. An embarrassing photo might not be the way you want people to remember you!

### THINK, THEN WRITE

**TIPS FOR SUCCESS**

Networking online uses written communication. You can prepare your comments in your own time without any pressure. Always think about how the things that you post will affect others. This means that you shouldn't be negative about others, or write anything that you wouldn't say in person. If you write something and then change your mind, you can delete the post.

# BUILDING A PROFILE

Social networking online is one of the most popular and effective ways of networking today. When you meet someone, you can look them up online, connect with them, and keep in touch. People can see your online profile, too. Here are some ways to make sure they are impressed with what they see!

## Be Prepared

The "About You" section of your online profile is a way to tell the world about you. Think about who you really are and try to communicate that in your profile. Tell people what your interests are, what your likes and dislikes are, and any other information that could help people to get a picture of the type of person you are. By being genuine, you'll attract people who have a lot in common with you and you'll make a good impression—one of the key tools in networking!

The Internet is part of our everyday lives, so your online profile is important.

14

Connect with other fans by sharing your love of music online.

## Online Footprint

Your online profile also includes all of the comments you have posted and things you have linked to. This means that someone can look at what you have written and shared and use that information to learn about you. It is important to interact online in a friendly way, just as you would face to face.

### POSITIVE IMPACT

**TIPS FOR SUCCESS**

Taking part in conversations online is a fantastic way to build a positive online profile. Think carefully about how to contribute relevant thoughts and ideas. You can always write a draft first, to check your spelling and grammar if you're unsure.

# ONLINE CONVERSATIONS

There are lots of different ways of using the Internet to communicate. You can post status updates about what you are doing, comment on other people's posts, and link to other sites, such as blogs or photo-sharing sites. The possibilities for networking on the Internet are endless!

## Who You Really Are

A blog is a fantastic way of sharing your ideas. If you link your writing to what is happening in your local area or something featured on the news, people are likely to take an interest. Blogs tell others about your skills and knowledge—what a wonderful way of networking! There are sites such as Kidblog that are specifically designed for kids who want to blog. Remember, though, it's always a good idea to tell your parents what you're posting before you put it online.

Sharing photos is a great way to capture memories and have fun.

**WARNING**

If an online conversation upsets you in any way, be sure to tell your parents or another trusted adult.

# Give a Response

Most social networking websites allow people to comment when something is posted. This can often be the beginning of a conversation with others, and it may even lead you to new interests and ideas. Remember that comments can be viewed by others, so always be polite and respectful. Be sure you use sites that are designed for young people, and always let your parents know what you're doing online.

## TIPS FOR SUCCESS

### ASK PERMISSION

If you have a photo or a blog that shows or mentions another person, remember to ask for permission before you post it. Perhaps the person would rather you didn't include him or her. He or she might not want you to use their name. Everyone's online profile is personal, so be careful not to upset people by doing something they might not want you to.

Online networking sites allow you to interact safely with other kids.

# NETWORKING FACE-TO-FACE

Networking face-to-face is as important as networking online. Once you've found some good places to network offline, what do you do when you're there? Having conversations in person can often be harder than online, but once you get used to it, there can be nothing better than making that personal connection with someone!

## Remember to Smile

"Smile and the world smiles with you," or so the saying goes. If you smile at people, they are likely to smile back. A friendly, smiling face is far more approachable than a face with a miserable or bored expression! Smiling is a signal that you are approachable and willing to talk, and it's the best way to start a conversation. Once you have made eye contact and given a friendly smile, beginning to chat is much easier.

When you meet up with a friend, you make eye contact and smile.

Networking is about relaxing and having fun.

## Show an Interest

Learning how to ask questions is an important networking skill. Most people respond well if you show an interest in them. If you ask their opinions and listen to what they say, they will feel that you value their ideas. Remember to pay attention to what they are telling you and respond by asking further questions as a way of finding out more. If you are shy, it can be tempting to speak quietly or mumble. However, you should always try to speak clearly, so people can understand what you're saying.

### MAKING SENSE

When you are talking to people about your interests, remember that they might have little or no knowledge of the subject. Keep your explanations simple, rather than overwhelming the other person with facts. Showing enthusiasm is vital—this is what people are likely to remember about you.

**TIPS** FOR **SUCCESS**

# PRACTICE MAKES PERFECT

Some people are scared by the idea of talking to people they do not know. If that is how you feel, don't worry, it's natural. Having conversations is something that you can easily practice. And the more you practice, the easier it will become!

## Be Prepared

Starting a conversation is not always easy, especially if you have not met the other person before. Why not think of some questions in advance? If you join a sports club, you could ask others how long they have been playing a sport, or which professional player they admire most. Also guess what questions people might ask you, and prepare answers so you can respond.

Practice networking first with your friends. Ask them for feedback to help improve your conversation skills.

It pays to spend time working on networking skills. If you ask great questions, you are more likely to capture someone's attention.

## Among Friends

If talking to people worries you, first start by making conversation with your friends. If you have a new interest, try telling them about it. Once you are confident that you can speak to your friends, do the same with someone you haven't met before. Remember, the other person might be nervous, too!

### ELEVATOR PITCH

**TIPS FOR SUCCESS**

Explaining your ideas to other people can be difficult. Imagine you have an idea for a movie and you find yourself in an elevator with a director. You only have the time it takes for the elevator to reach its destination to convince him or her how exciting and original your idea is! In the movie business, this scenario is known as an "elevator pitch." It's a tough exercise, but a really useful one!

# DO YOUR RESEARCH

Networking is a great way of getting involved and learning from others. However, sometimes it can feel overwhelming. The good news is by doing a little research in advance, you will find it easier to network. Research will arm you with lots of fascinating facts you can use in your networking conversations.

## Be a Know-It-All!

Learning about things that interest you requires good research. To research well, think of yourself as a detective—it is up to you to find out everything you can about your subject. You must leave no stone unturned! Reading books, watching television documentaries, and searching for information online are all useful ways of researching a topic. The more you know about a subject, the more you'll have to say in conversation with other people when you begin to network.

Computers and books are a great place to research your favorite topics.

22

## Join the Conversation

Networking conversations can be easier if you already know a little bit about your topic. If you are going to listen to a presentation, find out some facts about the speaker and the subject. Carrying out some research in advance will help you get the most out of the presentation. You might even think of some questions to ask at the end. Don't be afraid to use the opportunity to introduce yourself to the speaker. You could tell them what you found interesting about the presentation and even ask them for advice. Don't worry if you don't feel confident enough to do this yet. Every step toward your goal, no matter how small, is taking you in the right direction.

### WRITE IT DOWN

**TIPS FOR SUCCESS**

If you are carrying out research before an event, remember to take notes as you work. It's easy to forget things when reading lots of information. If you have taken notes, you can look back at them if you forget what you have read, to jog your memory. Always remember to keep your parents informed of your networking plans, too.

# KEEPING IN TOUCH

Networking is about meeting people and sharing ideas. It works best if you build on the connections you make by developing friendships with the people you meet. Fortunately, there are lots of ways to do this, and staying in contact with people online is one of the most popular.

## Continue the Conversation

Taking notes is useful for keeping track of who you meet, and those notes will be really useful if you decide to keep in touch. Sending a message is a good place to start. Tell the person how great it was to meet them and, if you can, ask them a question. That will give them the perfect opportunity to respond to your message.

Sending a text message is just one way of making contact.

Teams and groups are great for building friendships.

## Give and Take

People often use networking as a way of gaining access to opportunities. However, networking is about much more than simply getting something you want. You will discover that there may be ways that you can help others, too. It is also worth keeping in touch with people even if they can't help you right now. They may be able to help you in the future.

### MORE THAN YOU

It can be tempting to always think about yourself first, but networking is about being generous and thoughtful. Show an interest in others and be a good listener—people will be there to listen to you when you need it, too.

TIPS FOR SUCCESS

# BUILDING YOUR NETWORK

Now you know what a network is, how to look for places to network, and how to make conversation. But what is your network useful for? A network is a wonderful resource. Here are some ways that building your network can help you.

Networks can be a wonderful source of support.

## Achieve Your Goals

A positive network is made up of people who know you and like you. They should be eager to help you whenever they can, just as you will help them. A network of people will support you when you are trying to achieve something, whether it is a sponsored run or a science competition. People in your network will also be happy to share their network with you. They might not be able to help you achieve your goals, but maybe they know someone who can, and would be willing to introduce you to that person.

Use your network as a way to discover fun things to do.

## Find New Opportunities

Networking is a fantastic way to find out what's going on. You can read and hear about what other people are doing, see whether there are any opportunities for you, and find out about the latest crazes. New trends often become popular by word of mouth or by "going viral." If you have a large network, you are sure to hear about them!

### IN THE LOOP

**TIPS** FOR **SUCCESS**

Social media is useful for hearing about what people in your network are doing. If someone writes a post that interests you, use the site to make contact with him or her and find out more. Keep up to date with your online network to stay connected.

27

# KEEP ON NETWORKING

The ways that you use your network will change as you grow up, but the connections you make can last a lifetime. You may find you make friends through your network that will become friends for life. Networking never stops, and, as you gain confidence, you will find yourself networking without even trying!

## Into the Future

For adults, networking is a vital career skill. A professional network, made up of other people working in the same industry, is the key to finding out about developments, trends, and job opportunities. Your network will allow you to access opportunities, take on new roles, and work with people who have similar interests and goals to yours.

Don't be surprised if your network leads to some wonderful, perhaps unexpected, opportunities!

Don't forget
to network
face to face
as well as
online.

## Social Networking Tomorrow

The Internet is still young and, as time passes, the way
we use it is likely to change. Social networking is already
a huge part of our lives—it's changed the way we study,
work, and interact with other people. Today, the Internet
is a key element of how we network. Keeping up to date
with new developments in social media and technology
will be vital to successful networking in the future.
Imagine how wide-reaching our networks may become
as the Internet develops over the years to come!

### KEEPING ON TOP OF IT

As your network grows, you might find it
difficult to keep track of it. Think about what
your networking goals are and organize your time
so you can achieve them. Remember to keep notes
so you don't have to rely on your memory alone.

TIPS FOR SUCCESS

29

# GLOSSARY

**blogs** online sites for writing about your interests

**communication** exchanging thoughts and ideas with others

**community** a social group linked by something in common, such as location, culture, or heritage

**confidence** belief or trust, particularly in yourself

**enthusiasm** showing interest and eagerness

**goals** results or achievements you are aiming for

**hobby** an activity you take part in for pleasure

**networking** developing connections with others with the aim of being mutually helpful

**opinion** a personal attitude or judgement

**opportunities** chances to achieve something

**permission** being allowed to do something

**plagiarism** using or imitating someone else's ideas or words without their permission

**post** to place something online, such as text or a photo

**professional** relating to an occupation or job

**research** to investigate carefully

**respectful** showing consideration and awareness of something or someone

**skills** abilities, things you do well

**social media** websites used by large groups of people to share information

**social networking** sharing ideas with groups of contacts with shared interests

**trends** things that are currently very popular

# FOR MORE INFORMATION

## BOOKS

Engdahl, Sylvia. *Online Social Networking*. Farmington Hills, MI: Greenhaven Press, 2007.

Jakubiak, David J. *A Smart Kid's Guide to Social Networking Online*. Kids Online. New York, NY: PowerKids Press, 2010.

Schwartz, Heather E. *Safe Social Networking*. Fact Finders. North Mankato, MN: Capstone, 2013.

## WEBSITES

For a simple and safe blogging site, try Kidblog:
www.kidblog.org

At KidzWorld, you'll find a safe social networking site with plenty of features, such as blogging:
www.kidzworld.com

YourSphere is a global social networking site where kids can connect and interact:
www.yoursphere.com

# INDEX